Empowered Ventures: Business ideas for black women

By

Nancy P. Moore

Presentation

In the domain of business, where development meets assurance, there exists a strong power that has for quite some time been underrated and disregarded — the enterprising soul of black women. "Empowered Ventures: Business ideas for black women " is a jubilee of this soul, an aid that enlightens the way to progress, and a challenge to step into the macrocosm of bottomless conceivable issues.

This book is conceived out of the acknowledgment that black women bring a one-of-a-kind point of view, flexibility, and innovativeness to the business scene. While confronting foundational challenges, they have reliably transcended affliction, cutting out specialties, and making huge commitments to different enterprises. "Empowered Ventures" isn't simply an assortment of business thoughts; it's a demonstration of the strength, development, and splendour inherent in black women. As we set out on this excursion, we dig into a different embroidery of innovative open doors, perceiving that there is no one-size-fits-all methodology. From magnificence and health adventures that celebrate different articulations of excellence to earth-shattering tech arrangements that push the limits of development, every thought is made fully intent on tackling the special qualities of individuals of black women.

This book isn't just a manual for potential undertakings yet in addition a recognition of the strength and assurance that courses through the veins of people of colour business visionaries. It is a festival of the previous, an acknowledgment of the present, and a guide for a future where the pioneering tries of individuals of colour are recognized as well as embraced and intensified. "Empowered Ventures" is a challenge to think beyond practical boundaries, to seek after interests, and to make organisations that succeed monetarily as well as contribute emphatically to the local area and the world overall. It is a call to construct an inheritance, to rouse the future, and to break unreasonable impediments with immovable beauty and strength.

Go along with us on this enabling excursion, where the pages of this book unfurl a bunch of potential outcomes, lighting the enterprising fire inside and preparing for individuals of colour to make a permanent imprint on the universe of business.

Chapter 1:

The Power of Entrepreneurship

Business is an undertaking; an extraordinary excursion releases the maximum capacity of people and networks. With regards to people of colour, business ventures turn into a powerful power, a pathway to strengthening, and a way to rethink conventional stories.

1.1 The Meaning of Business for Dark Women

Black women have an interesting story formed by flexibility, cleverness, and an unyielding soul. Business turns into an incredible asset for revising this story. It offers a road for financial autonomy, empowering ladies to shape their fates, break liberated from limits, and reclassify their parts in the public arena. As we investigate the pioneering scene, we'll uncover the complex manners by which black women can use their assets to make fruitful endeavours.

1.2 Beating Difficulties and Utilising Strengths

Recognizing difficulties is the most vital move toward defeating them. This part digs into the deterrents that people of colour could experience in the enterprising excursion, whether they be fundamental, social, or individual. In any case, the accentuation stays on the innate qualities that exceptionally position black women for outcomes in business ventures. From flexibility and imagination to local area-building abilities, we investigate how these characteristics can be bridled to defeat difficulties and flourish in the business world.

1.3 Moulding the Business Landscape

People of colour business people are not only supporters of the business scene; they are draughtsmen of progress. This segment looks at the authentic setting of black women in business, exhibiting pioneers who have made ready for people in the future. By understanding the past, we can see the value in the present and decisively shape the eventual fate of business for black women.

1.4 The Interconnection of Personality and Business

Character plays an essential part in moulding the enterprising experience. We investigate what the diversity of being dark and female means for business techniques, promoting approaches, and systems administration. By embracing and praising these convergences, individuals of colour business people can construct organisations that reverberate genuinely with assorted crowds.

1.5 Exploring Open Doors and Building Bridges

Business is tied in with immediately jumping all over chances and building spans for future achievement. This part closes with a conversation on how individuals of color can distinguish and explore valuable open doors, both inside their networks and on a more extensive scale. It underlines the significance of joint effort, mentorship, and making networks that encourage development and strengthening.

As we set out on this investigation of the force of business, we welcome individuals of colour to perceive the groundbreaking potential inside themselves and to embrace the pioneering venture as an impetus for strengthening, development, and enduring effect.

Understanding the significance of entrepreneurship for black women

Business venture, for people of colour, isn't simply a business pursuit; a groundbreaking power reverberates on different levels, achieving monetary strengthening, social impact, and cultural change. To understand the meaning of business for individuals of colour, it is fundamental to dive into the nuanced layers of this effective excursion.

1. Monetary Strengthening and Independence

The business fills in as a vehicle for monetary strengthening, giving people of colour the independence to shape their monetary fates. By laying out and claiming organisations, they are liberated from customary work limitations, setting out open doors for abundance, amassing, and monetary freedom. This monetary independence benefits individual business visionaries as well as adds to the financial imperativeness of networks.

2. Reclassifying Jobs and Narratives

The meaning of business venture lies in its ability to rethink customary jobs doled out to black women. Generally obliged by cultural assumptions, business permits individuals of colour to challenge and reshape these stories. As pioneers and trendsetters, they oppose generalisations, demonstrating that they can succeed in any industry and use impact across different areas.

3. Tending to Incongruities and Making Opportunities

Business turns into an intense device for tending to foundational differences faced by people of colour. By laying out organisations, they effectively add to limiting monetary holes and setting out open doors for them and others inside their networks. These endeavours become encouraging signs, showing that achievement is feasible independent of cultural difficulties.

4. Social Impact and Representation

People of colour business visionaries assume a critical part in moulding social stories and impacting cultural discernments. Through their endeavours, they present different points of view, items, and administrations that add to a more comprehensive portrayal of the business world. Business turns into a method for social articulation, displaying the extravagance and variety of encounters inside the African American population.

5. Local Area Improvement and Social Impact

Business ventures are an impetus for local area improvement and social effect. Individuals of colour business people frequently start organisations that address major problems inside their networks, encouraging positive change. From setting out work open doors to supporting nearby drives, these endeavours become necessary parts of local area development, adding to the prosperity of the two people and neighbourhoods.

6. Heritage Building and Generational Wealth

Business venture gives a stage to individuals of colour to create enduring heritages and generational financial stability. By laying out fruitful endeavours, they make pathways for people in the future, offering motivation and substantial instances of what is attainable. This heritage-building part of business goes past individual achievement, adding to the drawn-out success of families and networks.

Understanding the meaning of business venture for people of colour includes perceiving its diverse effects — from monetary strengthening and social impact to local area advancement and heritage building. As we explore this investigation, it becomes clear that business is a powerful power, offering people of colour a way to succeed exclusively as well as contribute genuinely to the more extensive social and monetary scene.

Conquering Difficulties and Utilising Qualities in the Business World

The excursion of business ventures is innately difficult, and for individuals of colour exploring the business world, these difficulties can be especially nuanced. Be that as it may, understanding and conquering these impediments frequently uncover a repository of qualities exceptional to the encounters of people of colour. This part investigates the craft of dealing with difficulties directly, while decisively utilising intrinsic qualities to make ready for progress in the business field.

1. Recognizing Fundamental Challenges

People of colour business visionaries frequently experience fundamental difficulties established in verifiable predispositions and imbalances. From restricted admittance to money to variations in business potential open doors, recognizing these impediments is the most important move towards conquering them. By perceiving fundamental difficulties, business people can foster methodologies to explore these obstructions and add to destroying foundational imbalances.

2. Embracing Versatility and Adaptability

Versatility is a sign of people of colour as business visionaries. This segment investigates the manners by which versatility turns into a useful asset for conquering difficulties. Whether confronting monetary obstacles, market vulnerabilities, or cultural predispositions, the capacity to return and adjust is a significant strength. Embracing difficulties as any open doors for development turns into a vital technique in the pioneering venture.

3. Utilising Social Intelligence

The social knowledge implanted in the encounters of people of colour is an important resource in the business world. This part digs into how social mindfulness and awareness can be utilised to associate with assorted crowds, making items and administrations that reverberate truly. Individuals of colour business visionaries have an interesting skill to connect social holes, cultivating inclusivity and extending market reach.

4. Building Solid Help Networks

Exploring difficulties turns out to be more sensible when upheld by solid organisations. This part investigates the significance of building unions with guides, friends, and local area associations. These organisations give direction and mentorship as well as a stage for shared encounters, encouraging a feeling of fortitude and strengthening among individuals of colour business people.

5. Taking advantage of Imagination and Innovation

Imagination is a strong power in defeating difficulties. Individuals of colour business visionaries frequently offer a remarkable point of view of real value, motivating creative answers for complex issues. This part examines how taking advantage of imagination can be a competitive edge, whether in item improvement, promotion, or tending to functional difficulties.

6. Promotion and Breaking Barriers

People of colour business people are not simply in business for individual achievement; they frequently become advocates for foundational change. This part investigates how business turns into a stage for breaking hindrances and pushing for inclusivity. By showing others how it's done, business people add to a change in the business scene, cultivating conditions that engage people, everything being equal.

7. Adjusting Certainty and Humility

Certainty, combined with lowliness, is a sensitive equilibrium that upgrades a business visionary's capacity to explore difficulties. This part investigates how individuals of colour can tackle the force of self-assuredness while staying open to ceaseless learning. Finding some kind of harmony turns into a foundation for building flexibility and versatility.

As people of colour defeat difficulties in the business world, they all the while tapping into a rich embroidery of qualities. Perceiving and decisively utilising these qualities push individual accomplishment as well as add to a more comprehensive and dynamic enterprising scene. The excursion turns into a demonstration of the backbone and creativity intrinsic in people of colour, moulding a story of win over misfortune in the realm of business.

Chapter 2:

Niche Beauty and Wellness Ventures

In the realm of business ventures, the excellence and health industry remains a material of endless conceivable outcomes. For individuals of colour, this area turns into a stage to reclassify magnificence principles, celebrate social legitimacy, and deal with items and administrations that take special care of different necessities. Part 2 investigates the domain of Specialty Excellence and Health Adventures, divulging the potential for people of colour business visionaries to make organisations that improve actual prosperity as well as engage people to embrace their interesting characters.

1. Embracing Assorted Guidelines of Excellence

Specialty excellence and health adventures for people of colour rise above customary magnificence standards. This part digs into how business visionaries can embrace and celebrate assorted guidelines of magnificence, making items and administrations that provide food explicitly to the interesting requirements and inclinations of individuals of colour. From skincare to haircare, the accentuation is on engaging people to feel positive about their regular magnificence.

2. Arranging Social Credibility

Social credibility turns into a vital component in specialty adventures inside the magnificence and wellbeing industry. Individuals of colour business people have the open door to organise items that draw motivation from social roots, praising the wealth of legacy. This section investigates how credibility reverberates with buyers as well as separates organisations in an undeniably cutthroat market.

3. Advancing in Normal Haircare and Styling

Regular hair care has arisen as a lively specialty inside the excellence business, giving a road to individuals of colour to embrace and praise their normal surfaces. The section investigates the advancement likely in normal haircare and styling items, revealing insight into how business people can take advantage of this developing business sector by offering powerful, socially full arrangements.

4. Wellbeing Past the Physical

Specialty magnificence and health adventures reach out past the physical to envelop mental and profound prosperity. This part investigates how black women business visionaries can make comprehensive well-being encounters, from spa benefits that focus on unwinding to emotional well-being drives that advance generally speaking equilibrium. The emphasis is on sustaining prosperity at each level.

5. Customised Skincare Arrangements

The excellence business is progressively moving towards customised skincare arrangements. Black women business visionaries have the chance to advance here by making items customised to the particular skincare needs of people with shifting complexions and surfaces. This part examines the significance of inclusivity in skincare and how customization can be a strong driver of progress.

6. Building People Groups Around Health

Specialty excellence and health adventures give a stage to fabricate networks around shared values and well-being objectives. This segment investigates how business visionaries can cultivate a feeling of having a place among purchasers, making spaces where people feel seen, heard, and upheld in their health processes. Building these networks improves brand dependability and adds to the general prosperity of purchasers.

7. Pioneering Examples of overcoming Adversity in Excellence and Wellbeing

Rouse and direct yearning for business visionaries, this part features examples of overcoming adversity of people of colour who have won in the excellence and health industry. From making imaginative items to building persuasive brands, these accounts act as signals of motivation, exhibiting that enterprising achievement is feasible in this powerful and advancing area.

As we investigate Specialty Excellence and Health Adventures, the section welcomes people of colour business visionaries to take advantage of their imagination, praise their social legacy, and improve in a space that goes past feel to cultivate all-encompassing prosperity. The magnificence and wellbeing industry become a material for business ventures as well as a domain where people of colour can reclassify, celebrate, and enable people to embrace their extraordinary excellence and health ventures.

Exploring opportunities in the beauty industry with a focus on unique products and services

The excellence business is a material of innovativeness and development, offering a variety of chances for business people to reclassify guidelines and present exceptional items and administrations. For individuals of colour, this area turns into a powerful jungle gym to celebrate social legitimacy, take special care of different magnificence needs, and layout adventures that reverberate with an expansive range of shoppers. This section investigates the tremendous scene of chances inside the excellent business, accentuating the potential for people of colour business visionaries to cut out specialties with particular and socially full contributions.

1. Observing Social Authenticity

One of the vital open doors inside the excellence business lies in celebrating social legitimacy. Individuals of colour business people can make items and administrations that draw motivation from different social foundations. From cosmetics conceals that supplement a scope of complexions to hairdos that embrace normal surfaces, this part investigates how social genuineness addresses the issues of underserved markets as well as cultivates a more profound association with shoppers.

2. Haircare Developments for Assorted Textures

The haircare business is seeing a shift towards inclusivity, perceiving and commending the different surfaces of hair. This section investigates valuable open doors for people of colour business visionaries to enhance in the haircare space, acquainting items customised with various hair types and styles. From defensive styles to imaginative hair care plans, business visionaries can take advantage of the assorted necessities of their interest group.

3. Manageable and Moral Beauty

"Sensible excellence" alludes to style or appearances that can be controlled or modified to fit specific norms or inclinations, frequently through beauty care products, preparation, or design decisions. It infers that excellence can be overseen or controlled somewhat.

Then again, "moral excellence" relates to characteristics or activities that are thought of as upright, moral, or ethically excellent. It goes past actual appearances and dives into the domain of character, conduct, and trustworthiness.

While sensible excellence centres around outside appearances, moral magnificence accentuates inward characteristics and a moral way of behaving. The two ideas hold importance in various settings and social orders, adding to individual and cultural impressions of magnificence and goodness.

4. Comprehensive Magnificence Tech Solutions

The magnificence business is at the front line of mechanical advancements. People of colour business visionaries can investigate valuable open doors in comprehensive excellence tech arrangements, for example, virtual cosmetics attempt-ons that take special care of an assortment of complexions or computer-based intelligence-fueled skincare conferences customised to different requirements. This part examines the potential for incorporating innovation into magnificence adventures, improving client experience and commitment.

5. Customised Magnificence Experiences

Purchasers look for customised magnificence encounters that take care of their remarkable inclinations and requirements. This segment investigates potential open doors for individuals of colour business people to offer customised discussions, arranged magnificence boxes, or customised administrations. By understanding the singularity of every client, business people can make significant and fulfilling magnificence encounters.

6. Specialty Scent and Aroma Blending

The scent business offers an extraordinary space for development and individual articulation. People of colour business visionaries can investigate open doors in specialty aroma and fragrance mixing, making aromas that reflect social subtleties and individual preferences. This part gives bits of knowledge into the specialty of scent creation and the potential for laying out unmistakable brands in this specific market.

7. Magnificence Schooling and Empowerment

Engaging customers through magnificence instruction is a strong open door inside the business. People of colour business visionaries can lay out adventures that give items as well as proposition instructive assets, instructional exercises, and studios. This part investigates how magnificence instruction can encourage a feeling of strengthening and inclusivity among buyers.

As we investigate valuable open doors in the excellence business, the section urges people of colour business people to embrace their imagination, celebrate social variety, and present exceptional items and administrations that reverberate with an expansive crowd. By perceiving and utilising the tremendous potential inside the magnificence of business, business visionaries can reclassify principles, meet different excellence needs, and add to a more comprehensive and energetic excellence scene.

Wellness and holistic health businesses catering to diverse needs

The well-being business is developing past conventional methodologies, embracing comprehensive well-being rehearses that focus on the general prosperity of people. For people of colour business visionaries, this presents a chance to make adventures that take special care of assorted needs, perceiving the remarkable parts of well-being and health inside various networks. This part investigates the far-reaching scene of well-being and all-encompassing well-being organisations, featuring the potential for business people to offer comprehensive and socially full administrations.

1. All-encompassing Wellbeing Practices

All-encompassing well-being underlines the interconnectedness of the psyche, body, and soul. People of colour business visionaries can investigate potential open doors in comprehensive well-being rehearses that take care of assorted needs. This part digs into administrations like needle therapy, reflection, and energy mending, underscoring the potential for organisations to give extensive prosperity arrangements that reverberate with different social points of view.

2. Socially Comprehensive Wellness and Movement

The wellness business is encountering a shift towards inclusivity, perceiving different body types, capacities, and social inclinations. People of colour business people can investigate open doors in socially comprehensive wellness and development organisations. From dance classes that celebrate social practices to workout regimes intended for various body types, this section investigates how business people can make inviting spaces for people, everything being equal.

3. Wellbeing Retreats and Experiences

Well-being withdraws offer people a potential chance to disengage, restore, and centre around taking care of oneself. People of colour business visionaries can take advantage of the developing interest in socially comprehensive health withdrawals and encounters. This part examines the potential for making withdrawals that incorporate different mending rehearses, care procedures, and social festivals to take special care of an extensive variety of well-being needs.

4. Healthful Administrations with Social Sensitivity

Healthful administrations that embrace social responsiveness give a significant road to people of colour business visionaries. This section investigates valuable chances to offer dietary direction, dinner arranging, and wholesome training that line up with assorted social inclinations and well-being contemplations. Business visionaries can make altered wholesome administrations that address the one-of-a-kind necessities of various networks.

5. Psychological Well-being and Directing Services

The significance of psychological well-being is earning respect, and there is a developing requirement for socially skilled emotional wellness administrations. People of color business visionaries can investigate open doors in giving emotional well-being advice and support that recognizes the effect of social variables on prosperity. This segment talks about how organisations can make places of refuge for people to address psychological well-being worries with social awareness.

6. All-encompassing Magnificence and Health Products

Health stretches out to magnificence items that focus on comprehensive prosperity. People of colour business visionaries can investigate amazing chances to make excellent items mixed with regular fixings, advancing both physical and profound health. This section examines the potential for offering skincare, haircare, and body care items that line up with all-encompassing well-being standards and take care of assorted needs.

7. Integrative Wellbeing Clinics

Integrative well-being centres unite customary and elective well-being rehearses. People of colour business visionaries can investigate open doors in laying out centres that give a scope of administrations, from needle therapy and homegrown medication to customary clinical medicines. This segment investigates the potential for making comprehensive well-being spaces that take special care of different well-being methods of reasoning and practices.

As we investigate well-being and all-encompassing well-being organisations, this section urges people of colour business visionaries to embrace the variety of prosperity needs inside various networks. By offering comprehensive and socially resounding administrations, business people have the chance to add to an all-encompassing well-being scene that focuses on the interesting parts of individual prosperity and encourages a feeling of inclusivity and strengthening.

Chapter 3:

Creative Arts and Culture Enterprises

The universe of inventive expressions and social endeavours remains as an energetic material where individuals of colour business visionaries can wind around stories, celebrate variety, and add to the social embroidery of society. Section 3 investigates the unique open doors inside innovative expressions and culture, displaying the potential for business people to lay out adventures that express individual inventiveness as well as resonate with different crowds, commending the extravagance of social legacy.

1. Creative Articulation and Business venture

Creative articulation is a strong type of narrating and social portrayal. This segment dives into the valuable open doors for individuals of colour and business people to transform their inventive gifts into organisations. From visual expressions to execution expressions, business people can investigate roads like craftsmanship exhibitions, studios, or online stages to feature and sell their work.

2. Comprehensive developments and Celebrations

Comprehensive developments and celebrations give a stage to celebrate variety and unite networks. This section investigates the potential for business visionaries to sort out and organise comprehensive developments, exhibiting different artistic expressions, music, dance, and culinary encounters. By making spaces that celebrate social wealth, business people add to local area commitment and social trade.

3. Afrofuturism and Inventive Plan

Afrofuturism is a thriving classification that mixes African culture with cutting-edge components. People of colour business visionaries can investigate valuable open doors in imaginative plans and styles enlivened by Afrofuturism. This part examines how organisations can make and market items that mix social feel with present-day plans, from apparel and assistants to home style.

4. Distributing and Abstract Endeavours

The scholarly world offers material for narrating and social investigation. Business visionaries can dig into distributing and artistic endeavours, making stages for different voices and stories. This section investigates chances to lay out distributing houses, book shops, or scholarly occasions that enhance the voices of individuals of colour writers and narrators.

5. Social Legacy Conservation Activities

Protecting social legacy turns into a significant endeavour that interfaces with local area personality. People of colour business visionaries can investigate open doors in social legacy protection projects, going from narrative filmmaking to authentic drives. This part examines how organisations can effectively add to safeguarding and sharing social chronicles.

6. Advanced Media and Content Creation

The advanced age offers huge open doors for content creation and media creation. Individuals of colour business visionaries can use advanced stages to make and disseminate socially resounding substance. This section investigates the potential for laying out computerised media organisations, including webcasts, YouTube channels, or real-time features that celebrate different points of view.

7. Social Training and Studios

Social instruction turns into an integral asset for encouraging comprehension and appreciation. Business people can investigate amazing open doors in giving social training and studios, whether in schools, public venues, or online stages. This part talks about how organisations can add to social mindfulness and scaffold holes through instructive drives.

8. Joint efforts and Organisations

Joint efforts and organisations intensify the effect of social undertakings. This part investigates the potential for business visionaries to team up with specialists, associations, and powerhouses to make cooperative energies. By shaping significant organisations, organisations can extend their range and add to a more extensive social exchange.

As we investigate the domain of innovative expressions and social endeavours, this section urges people of colour business visionaries to embrace the groundbreaking force of workmanship and social articulation. By laying out adventures that celebrate variety, enhance social voices, and add to the innovative economy, business visionaries express their distinction as well as become impetuses for positive social change inside their networks and then some.

Unleashing creativity through art, design, and cultural entrepreneurship

investigates the powerful convergence of inventiveness, business, and social articulation inside the domains of craftsmanship and planning. For people of color business visionaries, this space turns into a material for self-articulation, a stage for social festivals, and a road to shape extraordinary stories that resonate with different crowds.

1. Engaging Voices through Visual Expressions

Visual expressions act as a strong vehicle for self-articulation and social narrating. People of colour business visionaries can release their imagination through craftsmanship exhibitions, studios, and online stages. This part investigates how organisations can engage specialists, give display spaces, and add to the more extensive social exchange through visual articulations.

2. Design Business venture and Social Character

Style turns into a strong type of social articulation. People of color business visionaries can investigate valuable open doors in style business ventures that celebrate social characters. This section examines how organisations can make clothing lines, frills, or stores that mix present-day plans with social impacts, cultivating a feeling of satisfaction and personality.

3. Planning Spaces and Encounters

The plan business offers roads for businesses that go past feel. Business visionaries can investigate valuable open doors in planning spaces and encounters that celebrate social variety. This segment investigates how organisations can add to establishing socially rich conditions, whether in an inside plan, occasion arranging, or vivid encounters.

4. Social Business venture in the Computerised Circle

The computerised scene gives vast potential outcomes to social business ventures. People of colour business visionaries can use online stages to grandstand and sell social items, contacting a worldwide crowd. This part talks about how organisations can lay out computerised commercial centres, web-based business stages, or take part in virtual entertainment to enhance social accounts.

5. Coordinated efforts with Social Powerhouses

Coordinated efforts with social powerhouses become an essential road for social business ventures. This segment investigates the potential for business people to collaborate with powerhouses, specialists, and social symbols. By framing significant joint efforts, organisations can take advantage of existing crowds and upgrade the perceivability of social articulations.

6. Distinctive and Carefully assembled Adventures

The resurgence of interest in distinctive and carefully assembled items presents open doors for social business ventures. People of colour business visionaries can investigate adventures that focus on making high-quality products, from adornments and materials to home style. This part examines how organisations can celebrate conventional craftsmanship while injecting contemporary components.

7. Social Business in Film and Media

Film and media offer strong channels for narrating and social portrayal. Business people can investigate open doors in social business ventures inside the domains of filmmaking, narratives, and media creation. This part digs into how organisations can add to moulding different accounts and enhancing social voices through visual narrating.

8. Inventive Hatcheries and Spaces

Laying out inventive hatcheries and spaces turns into an exceptional method for cultivating social business. This section investigates how business visionaries can make centres that help specialists, creators, and social pioneers. By giving assets, mentorship, and cooperative conditions, organisations can add to the thriving of innovative articulations.

As we explore the domain of craftsmanship, planning, and social business, this section urges individuals of colour as business visionaries to see their endeavours as organisations as well as social supporters. By releasing innovativeness, celebrating assorted articulations, and cultivating enterprising undertakings that intensify social accounts, business people become makers as well as the impetus for positive change inside the social scene.

Building businesses that celebrate and preserve cultural heritage

digs into the significant domain of business venture that goes past benefit age - organisations devoted to praising and saving social legacy. For individuals of color business visionaries, this space turns into an open door to communicate inventiveness as well as to add to the conservation and advancement of different social inheritances effectively.

1. High-quality Artwork and Customary Techniques

Business people can celebrate and save social legacy by laying out organizations that pay attention to distinctive specialties and conventional strategies. This part investigates valuable chances to make adventures that produce hand-tailored merchandise, keeping conventional abilities alive while offering one-of-a-kind, socially rich items to a worldwide crowd.

2. Culinary Endeavours Observing Social Cuisine

Food is a strong articulation of culture. Business visionaries can lay out culinary endeavours that celebrate and save social food. This part talks about the potential for organisations to offer conventional food varieties, cooking classes, or even lay out eateries that feature the wealth and variety of social culinary practices.

3. Social Training and Legacy Tours

Instructive endeavours that celebrate social legacy can appear as directed legacy visits, studios, and social drenching encounters. This segment investigates how business visionaries can make organisations that teach and illuminate people about social chronicles, customs, and relics, adding to a more extensive comprehension of different legacies.

4. Moral Style and Manageable Practices

Business people can add to the protection of social legacy by laying out design organisations that stick to moral and manageable practices. This part digs into how organisations can integrate conventional materials, examples, and craftsmanship while guaranteeing fair and economical creation strategies.

5. Language and Writing Initiatives

Saving social legacy includes protecting dialects and writing. Business people can make organisations that emphasise language conservation drives, including language learning stages, writing distributions, and narrating occasions that praise the lavishness of semantic variety.

6. Widespread developments and Festivals

Sorting out comprehensive developments and celebrations turns into a unique method for commending and safeguarding legacy. This part investigates valuable open doors for business visionaries to lay out organisations that host occasions, displaying different parts of social legacy, from expressions and specialties to music and dance.

7. Social Protection through Advanced Platforms

In the advanced age, business people can use online stages to add to social conservation effectively. This part examines how organisations can make computerised chronicles, virtual galleries, or instructive substances that guarantee the openness and life span of social legacy.

8. Coordinated efforts with Craftsmans and Social Practitioners

Coordinated efforts with craftsmans, social specialists, and conventional skilled workers become a cooperative way to deal with protecting social legacy. This segment investigates the potential for business visionaries to frame associations that commonly benefit organisations and social specialists, cultivating the continuation of customary expressions and specialties.

9. Social Legacy Protection Initiatives

Business people can lay out organisations that emphasise social legacy protection, including rebuilding projects, conservation endeavours, and drives that shield verifiable locales and antiques. This part examines how organisations can assume a functioning part in guaranteeing the life span of social fortunes.

As individuals of colour business people adventure into organisations that celebrate and safeguard social legacy, the section energises a comprehensive methodology that joins imagination, supportability, and local area commitment. By effectively adding to the protection of social inheritances, business people make practical organisations as well as become stewards of history, guaranteeing that different social legacies proceed to flourish and move ages to come.

Chapter 4:

Tech and Innovation Hubs

In the consistently developing scene of innovation and development, people of colour business visionaries have a one-of-a-kind chance to lay out centres that cultivate mechanical progressions as well as champion variety and consideration. Section 4 investigates the unique universe of Tech and Advancement Center points, where innovativeness, cooperation, and state-of-the-art arrangements cross to shape what's in store.

1. Exploring the Tech Scene with Innovation

Business people can explore the tech scene by laying out centres that focus on development. This part investigates how Tech and Development Centers can act as impetus for noteworthy thoughts, offering a space where different points of view add to the improvement of innovations that address certifiable difficulties.

2. Moving the Cutting Edge Through STEM Initiatives

Tech and Development Centers become stages for motivating the up-and-coming age of people of colour in STEM (Science, Innovation, Designing, and Arithmetic). This section digs into the potential for business people to make drives that give mentorship, schooling, and assets, encouraging a pipeline of different abilities in the tech business.

3. Hatching Tech New businesses with Variety Focus

Business people can lay out centre points that explicitly hatch tech new companies with an emphasis on variety and incorporation. This part investigates how organisations can give assets, mentorship, and financing to new businesses driven by individuals of colour, guaranteeing a more impartial portrayal inside the tech pioneering scene.

4. Spanning the Advanced Gap Through Tech Education

Tech and Development Center points can assume a vital part in crossing over the computerised partition. This section talks about amazing open doors for business visionaries to make instructive projects, studios, and drives that give tech education, guaranteeing that underrepresented networks approach the abilities required in an undeniably advanced world.

5. Variety in Tech Occasions and Conferences

Occasions and meetings held inside Tech and Advancement Center points become key drivers of variety and consideration in the tech area. This segment investigates how business visionaries can put together and have occasions that enhance assorted voices, feature inventive ventures, and set out systems administration to open doors that encourage joint effort.

6. Computer-based Intelligence and AI for Social Impact

The crossing point of man-made brainpower (computer-based intelligence) and AI presents potential open doors for business people to lay out centres with an emphasis on friendly effect. This part examines how organisations can use these advancements to address cultural difficulties, from medical care to schooling, guaranteeing that tech developments decidedly affect different networks.

7. Online Protection and Computerised Wellbeing Initiatives

As computerised innovations advance, guaranteeing online protection and computerised well-being becomes central. Business visionaries can lay out Tech and Development Centers that pay attention to network safety drives, including instruction, preparation, and arrangements that shield people and organisations from online dangers.

8. Blockchain and Fintech Innovation

Blockchain and fintech present groundbreaking open doors for business people in the tech space. This part investigates how Tech and Development Center points can become hatcheries for new companies that influence blockchain innovation and fintech advancements, adding to headways in monetary consideration and decentralised frameworks.

9. Making Tech Centers in Underserved Communities

Business people can have a massive effect by laying out Tech and Development Center points in underserved networks. This section dives into the potential for organisations to make centre points that give admittance to innovation, preparation, and enterprising assets, enabling people in underestimated regions to take part in the tech-driven economy.

As we investigate the universe of Tech and Advancement Centers, this part urges individuals of colour business visionaries to embrace the mechanical wilderness as well as effectively shape it. By cultivating development, rousing the future, and supporting variety inside the tech business, business visionaries can make centers that add to mechanical progressions as well as act as signals of incorporation and strengthening.

Navigating the Tech Landscape with Innovative Solutions

In the speedy domain of innovation, business people, particularly individuals of color, can have a massive effect by exploring the tech scene with creative arrangements. Section 6 investigates how innovativeness, versatility, and a groundbreaking outlook can be utilised to address difficulties, make significant changes, and add to the powerful development of the tech business.

1. Distinguishing Business Sector Holes and Opportunities

Business visionaries can explore the tech scene by distinguishing market holes and open doors. This segment investigates how a sharp consciousness of arising patterns, purchaser needs, and underserved markets can prompt the improvement of imaginative arrangements that address certifiable issues.

2. Embracing Arising Technologies

Remaining at the bleeding edge of arising advancements is fundamental for exploring the tech scene. This part digs into the open doors introduced by advancements like man-made reasoning, blockchain, and the Web of Things. By embracing these advancements, business visionaries can make arrangements that shape the eventual fate of different ventures.

3. Client-Driven Plan and Experience

Development in the tech business is intently attached to client-driven plans and experience. This segment investigates how business visionaries can focus on the requirements and encounters of end clients while creating items or administrations. By zeroing in on convenience and openness, creative arrangements can reverberate all the more actually with different crowds.

4. Utilising Information for Informed Decisions

Information-driven independent direction turns into an amazing asset for exploring the tech scene. This part talks about how business visionaries can use information investigation to acquire bits of knowledge, recognize examples, and pursue informed choices. Information-driven advancement takes into consideration the improvement of arrangements that are natural as well as receptive to changing business sector elements.

5. Building Cooperative Ecosystems

Exploring the tech scene frequently includes joint efforts and organisations. Business visionaries can make cooperative biological systems where various gifts meet up to ideate and improve. This segment investigates how building organisations, cultivating associations, and teaming up with different pioneers can enhance the effect of tech arrangements.

6. Supportable and Moral Tech Practices

Advancement in the tech business stretches out past usefulness to envelop maintainability and moral practices. This section talks about how business visionaries can explore the scene by integrating natural obligation, moral contemplations, and social effect into the centre of their tech arrangements, adjusting development to more extensive cultural objectives.

7. Nonstop Learning and Adaptability

The tech scene is described by steady development. Business visionaries can explore this unique climate by embracing persistent learning and flexibility. This segment investigates how remaining informed about industry patterns, partaking in proficient turn of events, and encouraging a culture of flexibility add to supported development.

8. Comprehensive and Various Tech Teams

Development flourishes in assorted and comprehensive conditions. This section dives into the significance of building tech groups that address different foundations, viewpoints, and encounters. Comprehensive groups add to a more extravagant pool of thoughts, encouraging development that reverberates with a different client base.

9. Pioneering Flexibility Notwithstanding Challenges

Challenges are intrinsic in the tech scene, yet pioneering strength turns into a vital factor in defeating them. This segment investigates how business visionaries can explore difficulties, gain from disappointments, and adjust their techniques to guarantee the proceeds with improvement of creative arrangements.

As people of colour business visionaries explore the tech scene with creative arrangements, this part energises a comprehensive methodology that consolidates innovative mastery with a pledge to social effect and moral practices. By cultivating advancement that is comprehensive, economical, and receptive to cultural necessities, business visionaries can prevail in the tech business as well as add to positive and enduring change.

Inspiring the next generation through STEM initiatives

In a time characterised by mechanical progressions and logical forward leaps, motivating the cutting edge to embrace STEM (Science, Innovation, Designing, and Math) is foremost. STEM drives go past customary instruction, offering a diverse way to deal with developing interest, innovativeness, and critical thinking abilities. This top-to-bottom article investigates the meaning of moving the cutting edge through STEM drives and dives into the different parts that make these projects extraordinary.

1. Interactive Growth opportunities:

STEM drives flourish with intuitive growth opportunities that rise above conventional study hall limits. Active exercises, examinations, and activities permit understudies to apply hypothetical information in genuine situations. This approach upgrades understanding as well as cultivates a feeling of interest and miracle.

2. Diverse Good examples:

Portrayal matters, particularly in fields where variety has generally been deficient. STEM drives effectively look to exhibit a different scope of good examples, underscoring the accomplishments of people from underrepresented gatherings. This openness furnishes youthful personalities with engaging figures, stalling generalisations, and rousing a more extensive range of trying researchers, specialists, and technologists.

3. Mentorship Projects:

Mentorship plays a crucial part in directing the cutting edge through their STEM processes. Laying out associations with experienced experts permits understudies to acquire bits of knowledge, guidance, and useful information. Mentorship programs make a steady organisation that sustains ability, offering a guide for individual and expert turn of events.

4. Real-World Applications:

Connecting STEM ideas to true applications is essential for rousing future trend-setters. STEM drives frequently integrate industry-pertinent activities, exhibiting the unmistakable effect of logical and mechanical progressions on society. This approach makes learning more captivating as well as features the potential for positive change through STEM tries.

5. Inclusive Schooling:

STEM drives focus on inclusivity, expecting to arrive at understudies from different foundations and shifting degrees of scholarly capability. By giving equivalent chances to learning and investment, these projects guarantee that nobody is abandoned. Inclusivity encourages a cooperative climate where alternate points of view add to all-encompassing critical thinking.

6. Encouraging Decisive Reasoning:

STEM instruction isn't just about remembering realities; it's tied in with developing decisive reasoning abilities. Drives centre around empowering understudies to address, dissect, and take care of issues freely. This approach ingrains a mentality of flexibility and versatility, fundamental characteristics for exploring the consistently developing scene of STEM disciplines.

7. Global Joint effort:

The interconnected idea of STEM fields accentuates the significance of the worldwide coordinated effort. STEM drives frequently integrate worldwide tasks, presenting understudies with different viewpoints and encouraging a feeling of worldwide citizenship. Cooperative endeavours widen skylines as well as set up the cutting edge for a reality where innovative arrangements are progressively interconnected.

Motivating the cutting edge through STEM drives isn't just about getting people ready for explicit professions; it's tied in with outfitting them with the abilities and mentality expected to flourish in a dynamic and innovation-driven world. These drives establish the groundwork for development, interest, and inclusivity, guaranteeing that the future innovators in STEM are different, good to go, and equipped for tending to the complicated difficulties that lie ahead. As we put resources into these drives, we make ready for an age that won't just hug STEM yet in addition reclassify and hoist its effect on society.

Chapter 5:

Social Impact Ventures

In the always-developing scene of business, Section 5 of our investigation digs into the domain of Social Effect Adventures. This section is a demonstration of the groundbreaking force of organisations that focus on both benefit and positive cultural change. Social effect adventures address a change in outlook, where the quest for monetary achievement is blended with a guarantee to tending to squeeze social and natural difficulties.

1. Defining Social Effect Ventures:

Social effect adventures, at their centre, are ventures driven by a double reason - monetary feasibility and a positive effect on society. These endeavours look for inventive answers to address issues like neediness, imbalance, and ecological debasement, and that's just the beginning. Part 5 reveals insight into the assorted structures these endeavours can take, underlining that benefit and object are not unrelated.

2. Business as a Power for Good:

The section highlights that organisations can be a strong power for good. It investigates contextual investigations and examples of overcoming adversity of adventures that have shown the way that a guarantee to social effect can drive development, draw in cognizant buyers, and make an economical plan of action. This shift difficulties conventional ideas of benefit-driven business ventures.

3. Measuring Impact:

A vital part of social effect adventures is the estimation of their effect. Section 5 gives experiences into different measurements and evaluation apparatuses used to check the adequacy of these endeavours. Understanding the subtleties of effect estimation is urgent for partners, financial backers, and the actual endeavours to guarantee responsibility and consistent improvement.

4. Collaboration and Partnerships:

Social effect adventures flourish with joint effort. The section investigates how associations with non-benefits, states, and different organisations can enhance the range and adequacy of these endeavours. The interconnected idea of social difficulties frequently requires an aggregate and cooperative methodology, and Section 5 features effective instances of such organisations.

5. Challenges and Opportunities:

While social-effect adventures contribute altogether to positive change, they additionally face novel difficulties. The part digs into issues like adaptability, financing imperatives, and the requirement for fundamental change. All the while, it features valuable open doors for development, advancement, and the possibility to impact more extensive cultural mentalities toward capable and feasible strategic policies.

6. Inspiring the Following Generation:

A vital subject in this part is the motivation these endeavours give to the up-and-coming age of business people. By displaying instances of organisations having a significant effect, Part 5 plans to light the energy of hopeful business people who look for monetary accomplishment as well as a reason-driven vocation that adds to a superior world.

7. The Eventual Fate of Social Effect Ventures:

As the part closes, it anticipates the eventual fate of social-effect adventures. It investigates arising patterns, developing plans of action, and the job of innovation in driving positive change. The section welcomes perusers to imagine a business scene where the social effect isn't simply a decision but an essential piece of the enterprising ethos.

In rundown, Section 5: Social Effect Adventures fills in as a manual for understanding, appreciating, and partaking in the developing development of organisations that focus on friendly and natural effects. Through contextual investigations, bits of knowledge, and provocative conversations, this section welcomes perusers to investigate the convergence of benefit and reason, provoking them to imagine an existence where a business venture turns into an impetus for positive change.

Creating businesses with a purpose: social enterprises, nonprofits, and community-driven initiatives

In the unique scene of present-day business, an outstanding movement is happening where organisations are progressively adjusting benefits to reason. This pattern is apparent in the ascent of social endeavours, philanthropies, and people who focus on local area influence over sheer monetary profit. This investigation digs into the different types of direction-driven plans of action and the significant effect they have on society.

1. Social Endeavours:

Social endeavours exemplify a plan of action where benefit age is interlaced with a guarantee to tend to social or natural difficulties. These endeavours focus on a "twofold primary concern," going for the gold achievement and positive cultural effect. Part 1 of our process divulges the complexities of how social undertakings explore the fragile harmony between supporting benefits and affecting the networks they serve.

2. Nonprofits:

Philanthropic associations, frequently determined by a mission to serve everyone's benefit, assume an urgent part in making positive change. Section 2 investigates the remarkable elements of charitable designs, featuring their dependence on gifts, awards, and volunteerism to satisfy their missions. It reveals insight into the difficulties charities face, underscoring the significance of key preparation and viable correspondence in accomplishing enduring effects.

3. Community-Driven People:

People enthusiastic for social change are instrumental in making organisations with reason. Part 3 spotlights the accounts of local area-driven people who start grassroots endeavours, missions, or private ventures that address explicit necessities inside their networks. These people act as motivating instances of how individual commitment can drive significant change on a nearby level.

4. Collaboration and Biological System Building:

A consistent idea through this investigation is the accentuation of cooperation. Sections 4 and 5 dive into how social ventures, not-for-profits, and local area-driven people can make strong biological systems by banding together with one another, companies, and government substances. This cooperative methodology intensifies their aggregate effect and resolves complex cultural issues all the more completely.

5. Measuring Effect and Straightforwardness:

Estimating the effect of direction-driven organisations is investigated in Section 6. Whether through measurements, appraisals, or stories, understanding and imparting this present reality impacts of these drives are vital for keeping up with straightforwardness and responsibility. The section stresses the job of effect estimation in building trust with partners and cultivating a culture of persistent improvement.

6. Challenges and Versatility:

Section 7 digs into the difficulties faced by organisations with a reason. From exploring monetary maintainability to dealing with the intricacies of social issues, these endeavours experience remarkable deterrents. Notwithstanding, the section additionally features accounts of strength, advancement, and flexibility, displaying how reason-driven organisations can defeat misfortune.

7. The Fate of Direction Driven Business venture:

As we finish up our investigation, Section 8 plans ahead. It imagines a scene where a reason-driven business venture isn't a special case but the standard. The part examines arising patterns, the job of innovation, and the developing assumptions for purchasers and financial backers, welcoming perusers to mull over the groundbreaking capability of organisations with a reason for moulding what's in store.

Generally, the excursion through making organisations with a reason unfurls as a mosaic of stories, difficulties, and wins. Whether from the perspective of social ventures, philanthropies, or local area-driven people, the story highlights the significant effect that reason-driven organisations can have on society, moving another age of business visionaries to coordinate benefit and reason for everyone's benefit.

The importance of giving back and building a socially responsible brand

In the present socially cognizant scene, the meaning of offering in return and laying out a socially capable brand goes past generosity — it's a key part of corporate personality and a strong driver for positive change. This investigation digs into the multi-layered motivations behind why coordinating social obligation into strategic approaches isn't simply a pattern but an extraordinary procedure.

1. Positive Effect on Networks:

One of the essential explanations behind offering back is the substantial and positive effect on networks. Socially dependable brands participate in drives that address neighbourhood or worldwide difficulties, whether through magnanimous gifts, local area activities, or associations. This inclusion encourages a feeling of corporate citizenship and positions the brand as a contributing citizen.

2. Building Trust and Faithfulness:

Shoppers progressively esteem straightforwardness and moral strategic policies. A socially capable brand acquires the trust of its crowd by showing a guarantee to social and ecological causes. This trust converts into client reliability, as customers are bound to help organisations that line up with their qualities and effectively add to making the world a superior spot.

3. Employee Commitment and Fulfilment:

Representatives are fundamental partners in the progress of any business. A socially capable brand draws in and holds top ability by giving a feeling of motivation past benefit. Drawing in representatives in volunteer projects or supporting causes they are energetic about makes a positive working environment culture, cultivating fulfillment and steadfastness among colleagues.

4. Long-Term Supportability:

Reasonable strategic policies are basic to a socially mindful brand. Whether it includes being harmless to the ecosystem processes, moral obtaining, or lessening carbon impression, these drives add to long-haul maintainability. Embracing supportability not only lines up with worldwide endeavours to battle environmental change yet in addition confirms the brand against developing purchaser assumptions.

5. Staying Significant in the Commercial Center:

As cultural qualities develop, buyers progressively look for items and administrations from brands that share their obligation to social obligation. Building a socially mindful brand isn't simply an ethical objective; it's an essential move to remain pertinent in a serious commercial centre. Organisations that disregard this perspective gamble on estranging a developing section of socially cognizant customers.

6. Meeting Administrative and Moral Guidelines:

Numerous enterprises are liable to elevated investigations concerning moral and mindful practices. By effectively partaking in friendly obligation drives, brands exhibit a pledge to fulfil or surpass administrative guidelines. This not only aids in keeping a positive public picture but additionally defends against legitimate and moral difficulties.

7. Inspiring all-inclusive Change:

By showing others how it's done, socially capable brands can move more extensive industry change. At the point when organisations exhibit the monetary reasonability and positive results of incorporating social obligation into their activities, they urge others to follow accordingly. This aggregate exertion makes a gradually expanding influence, encouraging a more mindful and moral business environment.

8. Contributing to Worldwide Objectives:

Socially capable brands frequently adjust their drives to worldwide maintainability objectives, like the Assembled Countries' Manageable Improvement Objectives (SDGs). By effectively adding to these more extensive goals, brands become a piece of a worldwide development toward a more fair, just, and maintainable world.

All in all, the significance of offering in return and building a socially capable brand reaches a long way past philanthropy — an essential basic effect of networks, buyers, and the drawn-out progress of the business. Embracing social obligation isn't just about what a brand does but about how it shapes its personality and adds to an existence where business is a power for positive change.

Chapter 6:

Professional Services and Consulting

In our investigation of different business scenes, Section 6 projects a focus on the unique domain of Expert Administration and Counseling. This area assumes a crucial part in supporting organisations across different businesses, giving master direction, key bits of knowledge, and specific arrangements. The part dives into the subtleties of this field, inspecting the difficulties, advancements, and extraordinary effect these administrations have on clients and the more extensive business scene.

1. The Advancing Scene of Expert Administrations:

The part starts by contextualising the developing idea of expert administrations and counselling. In a time set apart by quick mechanical headways and moving business sector elements, these administrations become key for associations looking for versatility, proficiency, and an upper hand.

2. Strategic Warning and Business Counseling:

A central part of expert administration lies in essential warning and business counselling. Part 6 investigates how specialists give important bits of knowledge, assisting associations with exploring intricacies, distinguishing potential learning experiences, and conquering difficulties. From the executives counselling to specific industry mastery, these administrations add to informed navigation.

3. Legal and Monetary Administrations:

Legitimate and monetary administrations become the overwhelming focus in the part, featuring the basic job they play in guaranteeing consistency, risk the board, and financial obligation. Whether it's legitimate guidance, monetary preparation, or review administrations, experts in this area add to the essential strength of organisations.

4. Technology Reconciliation and IT Counselling:

With the rising dependence on innovation, the part looks at how expert administrations stretch out to innovation coordination and IT counselling. Experts in this domain help organisations embrace and upgrade mechanical arrangements, improve effectiveness, and keep up to date with computerised changes.

5. Human Assets and Ability The board:

Individuals-driven administrations, like HR and the ability of the executives, are investigated concerning cultivating a positive and useful labour force. The section dives into how experts in this space add to enlistment, representative turn of events, and making a favourable work environment culture.

6. Challenges and Developments:

Each industry faces difficulties, and the expert administration and counselling area is no special case. The part investigates normal obstacles, for example, keeping up to date with mechanical headways, overseeing client assumptions, and adjusting to showcase changes. All the while, it features innovative methodologies that experts take on to defeat these difficulties and convey improved esteem.

7. Client-Driven Approaches:

Proficient administrations flourish with client fulfilment. The section digs into client-driven approaches, underlining the significance of understanding and addressing client needs. From customised counselling answers to encouraging long-haul connections, experts in this area are committed to conveying unmistakable worth to their clients.

8. Global Patterns and Future Possibilities:

As the section closes, it looks towards worldwide patterns forming the fate of expert administrations and counselling. Factors, for example, the ascent of remote work, expanded dependence on information examination, and the mix of man-made brainpower are investigated, offering experiences into how the area is ready to develop before very long.

Generally, Part 6 gives a complete investigation of the multi-layered universe of Expert Administrations and Counseling. By digging into the complexities of vital warning, legitimate and monetary administrations, innovation combination, HR, and client-driven approaches, the part offers a nuanced comprehension of how these administrations add to the achievement and versatility of organisations across businesses.

Excelling in the corporate world and leveraging expertise for consulting ventures

In the powerful scene of the corporate world, succeeding isn't just about ascending the various levelled stepping stools; it's an essential combination of abilities, connections, and a tireless quest for greatness. For those looking to rise above the bounds of customary business, utilising skills for counselling adventures is the way into a satisfying and prosperous profession. This article investigates the diverse ways to deal with success in the corporate space and consistently change into an effective counselling adventure.

1. Persistent Learning: The Groundwork of Greatness

Progress in the corporate domain starts with a guarantee of consistent learning. Embrace a development outlook, keeping up to date with industry patterns, innovative progressions, and arising best practices. Go to studios, seek postgraduate education, and look for mentorship to develop a profound and varied range of abilities. A balanced expertise portfolio improves your worth inside an association as well as turns into the bedrock for an effective counselling profession.

2. Compelling Correspondence: The Force of Impact

In professional workplaces, powerful correspondence is central. Improve your skill to convey complex thoughts in an unmistakable, brief way. Develop solid relational abilities, undivided attention, and flexibility in different correspondence styles. An ordering presence in gatherings, introductions, and composed correspondence pushes your vocation as well as lays out an establishment for drawing in counseling clients who are worthy of expressive and effective correspondence.

3. Building Solid Connections: Systems administration Dominance

Progress in any expert field is naturally attached to connections. Develop a hearty expert organisation inside and past your association. Effectively take part in industry occasions, courses, and systems administration stages to associate with friends, coaches, and expected clients. Building solid connections speeds up professional development as well as lays the foundation for a counselling adventure where references and verbal suggestions are priceless.

4. Influential positions: Exhibiting Skill

Take on positions of authority that permit you to exhibit your mastery. Lead projects, coach partners, and add to vital drives. Demonstrate your worth by conveying substantial outcomes and exhibiting a proactive way of dealing with critical thinking. These encounters not only lift your remaining inside the corporate ordered progression yet in addition give a convincing story to potential counselling clients looking for an old pro with a demonstrated history.

5. Individual Marking: A Stage for Counselling Adventures

As you succeed in your corporate excursion, foster areas of strength for a brand. Lay out an internet-based presence through stages like LinkedIn, exhibiting your ability, accomplishments, and thought initiative. A very much-created individual brand turns into a strong promoting device while progressing into counselling. Potential clients are bound to trust and draw in a particular and legitimate individual specialist brand.

6. Key Systems Administration: Exploring the Counseling Scene

While considering a shift to counselling, key systems administration becomes essential. Influence your current expert organisation and effectively look for associations in your objective counselling space. Go to industry-explicit occasions, take part in web-based gatherings, and team up with experts who supplement your abilities. Key systems administration opens ways to expected clients as well as gives experiences into market needs and serious scenes.

7. Customised Arrangements: The Counseling Edge

In the counselling domain, achievement relies on conveying customised arrangements. Use your corporate experience to distinguish specialty regions where your aptitude lines up with market requests. Create altered arrangements that address the extraordinary difficulties of your clients. Showing a profound comprehension of industry subtleties positions you as a significant expert fit for conveying unmistakable and effective outcomes.

Succeeding in the corporate world and consistently progressing into a fruitful counselling adventure is a nuanced venture. It requires a mix of ceaseless learning, viable correspondence, relationship-building, influential positions, individual marking, key systems administration, and the capacity to give custom-fitted arrangements. By decisively developing these components, experts can explore the unique corporate scene and influence their ability to lay out flourishing counselling adventures, opening new levels of expert and monetary achievement.

Establishing leadership in various professional fields

In the consistently developing scene of expert fields, laying out administration isn't restricted to a particular arrangement of abilities; a dynamic and versatile cycle requires a nuanced approach. Whether in business, medical care, innovation, or some other area, powerful authority is a general resource. This guide dives into the standards and procedures for laying out administration in different expert fields.

1. Visionary Authority: Outlining the Course

The initiative starts with a convincing vision. Fruitful pioneers across callings articulate a reasonable and rousing vision that directs their group or association. Foster a groundbreaking point of view, imparting a dream that resounds with your partners, and adjust your activities to the overall objectives. Visionary authority sets the establishment for outcome in any expert space.

2. Versatility: Exploring Change

In the present quick-moving world, flexibility is a sign of successful authority. Develop the capacity to explore change, embrace advancement, and lead your group through changes. Whether in money, medical services, or imaginative enterprises, pioneers who can adjust to developing conditions move certainty and encourage a strong hierarchical culture.

3. Powerful Correspondence: An Initiative Foundation

Independent of the field, viable correspondence is non-debatable for administration achievement. Foster solid verbal and composed relational abilities to convey thoughts, assumptions, and techniques. Effectively pay attention to your colleagues, cultivating an open and cooperative climate. Pioneers who succeed in correspondence assemble trust and work with strong collaboration.

4. Sympathy: Driving with Heart

In callings going from training to innovation, compassion is a key authority characteristic. Figure out the points of view and needs of your colleagues, clients, or patients. Pioneers who exhibit compassion establish comprehensive and strong conditions, cultivating reliability and upgrading general group execution.

5. Key Direction: Adjusting Dangers and Prizes

Authority frequently includes pursuing basic choices. Fostering solid scientific abilities and the capacity to weigh takes a chance against possible prizes. In fields like business and medical services, vital direction is instrumental in guiding the course of an association. Pioneers who make educated, determined choices add to long-haul achievement.

6. Helpful Group Building: Releasing Aggregate Potential

No matter what the expert field, building and driving successful groups is a foundation of initiative. Distinguish and sustainability, cultivate joint effort, and establish a climate that empowers individual development. Pioneers who move and engage their groups develop a culture of greatness and advancement.

7. Moral Authority: Directing with Trustworthiness

Uprightness is central in laying out authority across callings. Maintain moral guidelines, exhibit straightforwardness, and show others how it's done. Pioneers who focus on uprightness assemble trust inside their groups as well as with clients, partners, and the more extensive expert local area.

8. Nonstop Getting the Hang of: Remaining Ahead

Authority in any field requests a promise of ceaseless learning. Keep up to date with industry patterns, mechanical progressions, and advancing accepted procedures. Pioneers who put resources into their turn of events and energise a culture of advancing inside their groups position themselves as groundbreaking and fit for exploring the intricacies of their separate fields.

Laying out initiative across different expert fields requires a flexible range of abilities and a promise to immortal standards. Whether in business, medical care, innovation, or some other area, visionary administration, flexibility, compelling correspondence, sympathy, key direction, uplifting group building, moral lead, and ceaseless learning structure the bedrock of effective authority. By encapsulating these standards, experts might not just lead their groups higher than ever at any point but additionally make persevering through commitments to their picked fields.

Chapter 7:

E-Commerce and Digital Platforms

In the contemporary business scene, the seventh section of our investigation dives into the groundbreaking domain of Internet business and Advanced Stages. As the worldwide commercial centre goes through a change in outlook towards online corporations and exchanges, understanding the elements of Online business and utilising the force of computerised stages is urgent for organisations to flourish. This part unfurls the complexities of Web-based business, investigates the effect of computerised stages, and diagrams procedures for outcomes in the always-developing advanced commercial centre.

1. E-Business Development: From Blocks and Cement to Snap and Order

Follow the development of Internet business, from its modest starting points to its ongoing status as a foundation of worldwide exchange. Comprehend how organisations have progressed from conventional physical models to computerised retail facades, reshaping customer conduct and rethinking market elements. Investigate contextual analyses that feature fruitful Online business changes across enterprises.

2. Digital Stages: The Impetuses of Connectivity

Advanced stages have arisen as crucial empowering agents of business development. Research the job of stages like Amazon, Alibaba, and others in moulding the Online business scene. Look at how these stages work with consistent exchanges, offer strong calculated help, and deal with a commercial centre for organisations, everything being equal. Reveal the techniques utilised by effective business people in exploring and flourishing inside these computerised biological systems.

3. Consumer Conduct in the Computerised Age

Dissect the changes in purchaser conduct moved by the ascent of Online business. Investigate the comfort-driven buying designs, the impact of online surveys, and the effect of customised proposals. Acquire bits of knowledge into how organisations can adjust their procedures to line up with the assumptions and inclinations of carefully enabled buyers.

4. Challenges and Amazing Open Doors in E-Commerce

Inspect the difficulties faced by organisations wandering into the Internet business, including online protection concerns, planned operations intricacies, and the requirement for viable computerised showcasing. At the same time, dive into the bunch of open doors introduced by the computerised commercial centre, for example, worldwide reach, information-driven experiences, and creative income streams. Outfit perusers with an essential outlook to explore the Web-based business territory.

5. Building a Fruitful Online Business Strategy

Directing organisations toward progress in the computerised domain requires a hearty Web-based business system. Uncover the vital parts of a compelling system, including site enhancement, client experience configuration, secure instalment entryways, and consistent coordinated factors. Investigate contextual analysis representing how organisations have created and executed fruitful Web-based business systems, giving significant bits of knowledge to perusers.

6. Emerging Advancements in E-Commerce

As innovation keeps on progressing, investigate the effect of arising advances like man-made consciousness, increased reality, and blockchain on the Internet business scene. Research how organisations can use these advances to upgrade client encounters, streamline activities, and remain in front of the opposition. Outline reasonable instances of tech-driven advancements in Web-based business.

7. Regulatory Scene: Exploring Consistency in the Computerised Sphere

As Web-based business traverses worldwide limits, it is vital to grasp the administrative scene. Research the legitimate and administrative contemplations organisations should explore, including information insurance regulations, tax assessment issues, and consistency with worldwide exchange guidelines. Give a far-reaching manual for guaranteeing legitimate adherence while conveying Online business tasks.

In the last pages of Section 7, perusers will acquire a comprehensive comprehension of Web-based business and Computerised Stages, from their verifiable roots to the contemporary difficulties and potential open doors they present. Furnished with bits of knowledge into buyer conduct, viable techniques, and the advancing mechanical scene, organisations and business people will be exceptional to explore the computerised commercial centre and saddle the groundbreaking capability of Online business for supported achievement.

Tapping into the vast potential of online businesses

Taking advantage of the tremendous capability of online organisations requires an essential methodology that uses the computerised scene to its fullest degree. In this aid, we investigate key standards and noteworthy systems to assist business people and organisations with opening the open doors introduced by the internet-based domain.

1. Identifying Worthwhile Specialties: Accuracy Matters

Before sending off a web-based adventure, direct intensive statistical surveying to recognize specialty open doors. Search for holes on the lookout or regions with undiscovered interest. A designated and specialty-centred approach builds your potential for success of having out in a jam-packed web-based space.

2. Building a Solid Web-based Presence: Your Computerised Storefront

Put resources into an easy-to-use, outwardly engaging site that mirrors your image character. Enhance cell phones and guarantee a consistent route. A solid web-based presence lays out validity and gives a focal centre point to your crowd to investigate your items or administrations.

3. Effective Advanced Promoting: Perceivability is Key

Use computerised showcasing techniques to build perceivability and arrive at your interest group. Influence site design improvement (Search engine optimization), online entertainment showcasing, and content promotion to drive natural traffic. Paid publicising, for example, pay-per-click (PPC) crusades, can likewise help your web-based perceivability.

4. Embracing Online business Stages: Smoothing out Transactions

Consider utilising laid-out Web-based business stages like Shopify, WooCommerce, or Amazon to smooth out your Internet-based exchanges. These stages offer implicit devices, a prepared client base, and secure instalment passages, decreasing the intricacies related to setting up a free Internet business website.

5. Prioritising Client Experience: Maintenance Matters

Centre around conveying a remarkable client experience. Give clear item data, proficient client service, and a safe checkout process. Positive associations fabricate trust, empower rehash business, and produce positive informal, adding to long-haul achievement.

6. Harnessing Virtual Entertainment: Associating with Audiences

Probe the effect of arising advances like man-made knowledge,increased reality and blockchain on the internet business scene.Tailor your substance to reverberate with your objective segment, and use stages like Instagram, Facebook, or Twitter to grandstand your items/administrations. Online entertainment helps brand mindfulness as well as cultivates a local area around your business.

7. Data-Driven Independent direction: Examination Insights

Influence examination apparatuses to assemble experiences into client conduct, inclinations, and online execution. Information-driven navigation permits you to refine your techniques, streamline your web-based presence, and design your contributions in light of client patterns and criticism.

8. Seamless Portable Experience: Adjusting to Client Habits

Given the predominance of cell phone utilisation, guarantee that your internet-based business is advanced for portable stages. A consistent portable encounter adds to client fulfilment and grows your span to a more extensive crowd.

9. Innovative Advancements: Remaining Ahead

Investigate imaginative advances to improve your internet-based business. From man-made brainpower for customised client encounters to blockchain for secure exchanges, keeping up to date with mechanical headways can give you an upper hand.

10. Adapting to Patterns: Deftness is Key

The internet-based scene advances quickly. Remain dexterous and adjust to arising patterns. Whether it's new virtual entertainment stages, changing shopper ways of behaving, or mechanical headways, organisations that embrace change are better situated for supported achievement.

Taking advantage of the immense capability of online organisations includes an essential mix of market understanding, computerised promoting, client-driven rehearsals, and mechanical development. By embracing these standards and staying versatile to the developing internet-based scene, business people and organisations can lay out major areas of strength for a presence as well as tackle the boundless open doors the computerised domain brings to the table.

Strategies for success in the ever-evolving digital landscape

Exploring the steadily developing computerised scene requires a unique methodology and key mentality. Here, we investigate key procedures that organisations and experts can take on to make progress in the continually changing advanced climate.

1. Agile Transformation: Embrace Change

The computerised scene is set apart by quick advancement. Develop a coordinated mentality that embraces change as opposed to opposing it. Remain informed about arising patterns, advances, and purchaser ways of behaving. Organisations that can quickly adjust to new advancements are better situated for supported achievement.

2. Data-Driven Navigation: Outfit Insights

Information is a useful asset in computerised time. Execute hearty investigation frameworks to assemble experiences into client conduct, market patterns, and execution measurements. Settle on informed choices in light of these information-driven bits of knowledge, permitting your systems to develop in arrangement with genuine client needs and inclinations.

3. Digital Showcasing Authority: Perceivability is Key

A solid web-based presence is fundamental to the outcome in the computerised scene. Ace advanced showcasing channels, including web-based entertainment, content promoting, Web optimization, and paid publicising. Tailor your techniques to your ideal interest group and remain receptive to the always-changing calculations and best acts of every stage.

4. Customer-Driven Concentration: Focus on Client Experience

In the computerised domain, client experience is central. Focus on a consistent and natural client venture, from site route to checkout processes. Request and follow up on client criticism to improve and upgrade the general experience consistently. A fulfilled client is bound to turn into a brand advocate in the interconnected computerised world.

5. Innovation and Innovation Reception: Remain Ahead

Remain at the cutting edge of innovative progressions. Embrace creative innovations that can upgrade your business processes, further develop proficiency, and give an upper hand. From simulated intelligence and robotization to blockchain and computer-generated reality, understanding and incorporating these innovations can situate your business for progress.

6. Content Greatness: Instruct and Engage

Content remaining parts ruler in the computerised scene. Make superior grades, pertinent, and connect with content across different stages. Instruct your crowd, recount convincing stories, and lay out your image as a legitimate voice inside your industry. Significant substance constructs trust and cultivates long-haul associations with your crowd.

7. Strategic Associations: Work together for Growth

Fashion key associations inside the advanced environment. Work together with integral organisations, powerhouses, or industry pioneers. Key collisions can extend your scope, and acquire new crowds, and entryways to imaginative open doors that can drive outcomes in the advanced commercial centre.

8. Cybersecurity Watchfulness: Safeguard Your Assets

With expanded computerised collaborations comes an elevated gamble of network protection dangers. Focus on strong network safety measures to safeguard your business, client information, and online exchanges. Lay out a proactive network protection methodology to moderate dangers and fabricate entrust with your crowd.

9. Social Obligation and Straightforwardness: Assemble Trust

During a time of data, buyers esteem straightforwardness and social obligation. Convey your image values, maintainability endeavours, and moral strategic policies. Building entrust through straightforwardness can prompt more grounded associations with your crowd and positive brand discernment.

10. Continuous Learning: Develop a Development Mindset

The computerised scene is an interminable learning climate. Develop a development mentality inside your group, empowering constant learning and expert turn of events. Remain inquisitive, put resources into preparing projects, and cultivate a culture of versatility to explore the developing computerised scene.

The outcome of the consistently developing computerised scene requests a mix of versatility, key reasoning, client centricity, and mechanical sharpness. By embracing change, utilising information, dominating computerised promoting, focusing on the client experience, and remaining imaginative, organisations can get by as well as flourish in the dynamic and interconnected universe of advanced business.

Chapter 8:

Health and Fitness Entrepreneurship

In Part 8, we dive into the powerful domain of the Wellbeing and Wellness Business venture, investigating the extraordinary difficulties and opening doors inside this expanding industry. From the imaginative well-being of new companies to laid-out wellness marks, this section explores the pioneering scene of well-being and wellness, offering bits of knowledge and procedures for progress.

1. Market Elements: Wellbeing Popular

Investigate the advancing scene of well-being and wellness. Break down the rising customer mindfulness and interest in health arrangements, enveloping wellness, sustenance, emotional well-being, and all-encompassing prosperity. Understanding the market elements makes way for business people to likewise distinguish specialty potential open doors and design their contributions.

2. Imaginative Wellness Arrangements: Past the Rec centre

The cutting-edge well-being and wellness business visionary goes past conventional exercise centre models. Reveal imaginative wellness arrangements, including virtual exercises, customised preparing applications, and well-being withdrawals. Feature contextual analyses of business visionaries who have upset the business by reclassifying how individuals draw in with well-being and wellness.

3. Innovation Joining: From Wearables to Computer-generated Reality

Investigate the job of innovation in well-being and wellness business ventures. From wearable gadgets that track wellness measurements to vivid computer-generated simulation encounters for exercises, business people are utilising innovation to upgrade client commitment, personalization, and general health encounters.

4. Sustenance and Health Brands: Past Enhancements

Jump into the universe of sustenance and well-being brands, investigating the ascent of utilitarian food sources, dinner arranging applications, and customised nourishment administrations. Examine fruitful innovative endeavours that have taken advantage of the developing interest for items and administrations that advance all-encompassing wellbeing.

5. Emotional Well-being and Health: Tending to the Entire Self

Recognize the developing significance of emotional well-being and health in the business. Investigate enterprising endeavours that emphasise on pressure the board, care, and mental prosperity. Exhibit the effect of these drives on by and large well-being and how business visionaries are breaking marks of disgrace related to emotional well-being.

6. Building People Group: The Force of Association

Analyse the meaning of the local area working in wellbeing and wellness business. From wellness classes to online networks, business visionaries are making spaces where people can associate, share encounters, and back each other on their well-being processes. Exhibit the effect of local area expanding on client unwaveringly and business achievement.

7. All-encompassing Health Withdraws: A Developing Pattern

Uncover the ascent of all-encompassing well-being withdraws as an exceptional specialty inside the well-being and wellness business venture. Investigate how business people are arranging vivid encounters that consolidate wellness, sustenance, care, and unwinding. Feature fruitful models and the business procedures behind this well-being withdrawal.

8. Challenges in Wellbeing Business: Guideline and Morals

Address the difficulties faced by well-being and wellness business people,

including exploring administrative structures and keeping up with moral principles. Investigate how business visionaries can proactively address these difficulties to fabricate trust with customers and lay out a strong starting point for long-haul achievement.

9. Scaling Wellbeing and Wellness Adventures: Systems for Development

Dig into techniques for scaling wellbeing and wellness adventures. Investigate organisations, diversify models, and venture into developing business sectors. Feature business visionaries who have effectively scaled their organisations while keeping a promise to well-being and health standards.

10. Future Patterns: Remaining On the ball

Close the section by investigating future patterns in well-being and wellness business ventures. From headways in wearable innovation to arising health ideas, business people should remain on top of things to stay important. Examine how a pioneering mentality that embraces development can situate people for progress in the always-advancing well-being and wellness scene.

Section 8 gives an exhaustive investigation of the well-being and Wellness Business, offering a nuanced comprehension of market elements, inventive arrangements, innovation combinations, and the all-encompassing way to deal with health. Business people here, furnished with bits of knowledge from effective endeavours and a consciousness of arising patterns, are ready to have a tremendous effect on the prosperity of people and the eventual fate of the business.

Promoting health and wellness through fitness-related businesses

Advancing well-being and health through wellness-related organisations includes something other than offering workout schedules — it requires a comprehensive methodology that addresses physical, mental, and profound prosperity. In this aid, we investigate techniques for business visionaries to assemble organisations that support wellness as well as add to generally speaking well-being and health.

1. Tailoring Work out schedules: Personalization Matters

Plan workout schedules that take special care of individual requirements and objectives. Whether it's customised exercise plans, nourishment direction, or designated health techniques, fitting projects improve viability and cultivate a feeling of association among clients and their wellness process.

2. Incorporating Comprehensive Wellbeing: Past Actual Exercise

Extend past customary wellness contributions by consolidating comprehensive well-being parts. Incorporate care rehearses, stress decrease strategies, and sustenance schooling. By tending to the total prosperity of people, your business can have a more significant effect on their well-being.

3. Creating People group: The Force of Support

Construct a local area around your wellness-related business. Encourage a feeling of having a place and shared help among clients. Whether through in-person classes or online stages, a steady local area improves inspiration and assists people with remaining focused on their well-being and wellness objectives.

4. Utilising Innovation: Upgrading Accessibility

Influence innovation to make well-being and health available. Offer virtual exercise meetings, make an easy-to-use application for at-home activities, or give online assets to dietary direction. Innovation expands the scope of your business, making well-being and health administrations accessible to a more extensive crowd.

5. Educational Studios: Enabling Clients

Have studios and instructive meetings that provide clients with information about wellness, sustenance, and by and large prosperity. Informed clients are bound to go with feasible way of life decisions, adding to their drawn-out well-being.

6. Collaborations with Health Experts: Thorough Care

Work together with wellbeing experts like nutritionists, emotional well-being specialists, and physiotherapists. Offering a far-reaching way to deal with well-being guarantees that clients get balanced care that goes past wellness schedules.

7. Promoting Emotional well-being: Brain Body Connection

Feature the emotional well-being advantages of actual work. Integrate exercises that advance pressure decrease, care, and unwinding. Convey what ordinary activity emphatically means for mental prosperity, adding to pressure the executives and generally speaking satisfaction.

8. Sustainability Drives: Sound Planet, Solid People

Coordinate supportability in your wellness-related business. Accentuate eco-accommodating practices, from using green offices to advancing open-air exercises. A pledge to supportability lines up with comprehensive well-being and reverberates with clients who focus on both individual and natural well-being.

9. Corporate Wellbeing Projects: Expanding Impact

Offer corporate wellbeing projects to organisations hoping to put resources into the soundness of their workers. Tailor wellness and wellbeing drives for working environments, encouraging a culture of wellbeing that reaches out past individual clients to whole associations.

10. Measuring and Observing Achievement: Achievements Matter

Execute a framework to quantify client progress and celebrate achievements. Perceiving accomplishments, whether large or small, supports a positive way of behaving and persuades people to proceed with their well-being and health ventures.

Advancing well-being and health through wellness-related organisations includes a multi-layered approach that reaches out past actual activity. By fitting projects, integrating comprehensive well-being works, building a strong local area, utilising innovation, and cultivating joint efforts, business visionaries can make organisations that add to wellness as well as improve general prosperity, enabling people to carry on with better and more joyful existences.

Navigating the growing market for health-conscious consumers

Exploring the developing business sector for well-being cognizant buyers requires an essential methodology that lines up with developing patterns and increased consciousness of prosperity. Here, we investigate key methodologies for organisations hoping to take advantage of this expanding market and take special care of the requirements of well-being cognizant customers.

1. Understanding Purchaser Patterns: Informed Choice Making

Keep up to date with current well-being and health patterns. From plant-based diets to customised wellness schedules, understanding shopper inclinations permits organisations to tailor their contributions to line up with the most recent well-being cognizant requests.

2. Transparency in Item Data: Building Trust

Wellbeing cognizant purchasers esteem straightforwardness. Give nitty gritty data about your items or administrations, including fixings, obtaining, and dietary substances. Building trust through straightforward correspondence encourages dependability among shoppers who focus on understanding what they consume.

3. Offering Natural and Normal Decisions: Meeting Preferences

Take special care of the interest in natural and normal items. Whether in the food business or well-being administrations, giving choices liberated from fake added substances and synthetic compounds requests to wellbeing-cognizant customers looking for cleaner and healthier decisions.

4. Personalization: Fitting to Individual Needs

Embrace personalization in your items or administrations. Wellbeing cognizant buyers value fitted arrangements that take care of their particular necessities and objectives. This could incorporate customised sustenance plans, wellness regimens, or health programs intended for individual inclinations.

5. Incorporating Innovation: Upgrading Accessibility

Use innovation to make well-being cognizant contributions more available. From wellness applications to online stages for dietary direction, innovation expands the range of your business, making well-being-cognizant items and administrations accessible to a more extensive crowd.

6. Engaging in Friendly Obligation: Past Profit

Exhibit your obligation to social obligation. Wellbeing cognizant shoppers frequently line up with organisations that focus on moral obtaining, maintainability, and local area prosperity. Participating in drives that add to everyone's benefit reverberates with customers who look for brands with a feeling of direction.

7. Educational Advertising: Engaging Consumers

Teach purchasers about the medical advantages of your items or administrations. Give content that makes sense of the health benefits, wellness benefits, or in general prosperity commitments of what you offer. Enabling purchasers with information improves their trust in your image.

8. Community Building: Cultivating Connections

Make a local area around your image. Whether through web-based entertainment gatherings, occasions, or online discussions, encouraging associations among well-being cognizant customers advances the brand unwaveringly and gives a stage to shared encounters and backing.

9. Adaptability: Developing with Shopper Needs

Remain versatile to developing shopper needs. The well-being cognizant market is dynamic, with inclinations and patterns ceaselessly evolving. Organisations that can turn and adjust to these movements are better situated for supported achievement.

10. User Audits and Tributes: Building Credibility

Support and exhibit client surveys and tributes. Positive criticism from fulfilled clients constructs believability and trust. Wellbeing cognizant customers frequently depend on the encounters of others while coming to conclusions about health items or administrations.

Exploring the developing business sector for well-being cognizant shoppers requires an all-encompassing methodology that coordinates straightforwardness, personalization, innovation, social obligation, schooling, local area building, versatility, and validity. By lining up with the qualities and inclinations of well-being cognizant purchasers, organisations can flourish in this prospering business sector and add to the prosperity of their clients.

Chapter 9:

Real Estate and Property Ventures

Land, a dynamic and complex industry, becomes the dominant focal point in Part 9 of our far-reaching guide. This section dives into the complexities of land and property adventures, offering an abundance of information for both prepared financial backers and newbies to the field.

Market Patterns and Elements

Understanding business sector patterns is vital in the always-changing scene of land. Part 9 gives users a profound jump into current market elements, investigating variables, for example, market interest, loan fees, and financial pointers. By getting a handle on these patterns, financial backers can go with informed choices, distinguishing rewarding open doors and likely dangers.

Speculation Procedures

Compelling venture procedures are the foundation of outcomes on land. The part talks about different methodologies, from conventional strategies like long-haul property possession to additional cutting-edge procedures, for example, land crowdfunding. Perusers gain bits of knowledge into broadening, risk the board, and the significance of adjusting speculation objectives to economic situations.

Lawful Contemplations

Exploring the lawful parts of land exchanges is vital. Section 9 carefully covers key lawful contemplations, including property freedoms, agreements, and drafting guidelines. Understanding the legitimate system guarantees that financial backers can manage exchanges without a hitch and moderate likely lawful traps.

Property Valuation

Exact property valuation is an expertise each land financial backer should dominate. This part investigates different valuation systems, from the near market examination

(CMA) to the pay approach and cost approach. Furnished with this information, perusers can survey the genuine worth of a property, supporting fair dealings and informed speculation choices.

Property The Executive Procedures

Proficient property on the board is a key part of a fruitful land portfolio. Part 9 gives useful guidance on overseeing properties successfully, covering occupant relations, support, and managing unanticipated difficulties. Whether one possesses a solitary family home or a different business portfolio, this part offers important experiences for upgrading property execution.

Risk Moderation

Land adventures are not without dangers, and Part 9 diagrams procedures to alleviate these difficulties. From the exhaustive reasonable level of effort before buying a property to executing risk-the-board plans, perusers figure out how to shield their speculations against market instability and startling occasions.

Functional Insight for All Financial Backers

Whether perusers are prepared to land magnates or learners making their most memorable strides, Section 9 offers reasonable insight. True models, contextual investigations, and master counsel improve the story, giving an all-encompassing comprehension of the land scene.

All in all, Part 9 fills in as a far-reaching guide for anybody looking for progress in land and property adventures. By investigating market patterns, speculation techniques, lawful contemplations, property valuation, board procedures, and hazard relief, perusers are exceptional to explore the intricacies of this unique industry. Whether expecting to construct a different portfolio or upgrade existing speculations, the experiences from Part 9 proposition a guide to outcome in the steadily developing universe of land.

Building wealth through real estate investments and property management

Land has for some time been viewed as a strong vehicle for creating financial momentum, and keen financial backers have perceived its true capacity for producing significant returns after some time. Section 9 of our aid dives into the methodologies and standards behind creating financial momentum through land ventures and compelling property on the board.

Key Land Speculations

Putting resources into land includes something other than buying a property; it requires an essential methodology. The section investigates the idea of key money management, underlining the significance of careful statistical surveying, figuring out neighbourhood drifts, and distinguishing open doors for development. Whether it's private, business, or investment properties, going with very educated venture choices is critical to building a vigorous land portfolio.

Utilising Supporting and Tax reductions

Part 9 additionally reveals insight into the monetary parts of land speculations. Utilising supporting choices, understanding home loan terms, and using tax reductions are necessary parts of establishing financial stability through the land. Perusers gain experience in how savvy monetary arranging can upgrade returns and limit chances, establishing a positive climate for long-haul abundance gathering.

Property Appreciation and Income

The land offers double roads for abundance collection: property appreciation and income. The section analyses these ideas, outlining how vital property determination and powerful administration can prompt significant value increase over the long run. All the while, creating positive income from investment properties adds to progressing revenue sources, encouraging monetary soundness and development.

Compelling Property The executives

Fruitful establishing long-term financial stability in land relies on the successful property of the executives. Part 9 gives perusers pragmatic direction on overseeing properties proficiently. From occupant relations and rent arrangements to routine upkeep and tending to unanticipated difficulties, understanding the complexities of property the executives is vital. All around oversaw properties hold their worth as well as contribute fundamentally to general speaking portfolio development.

Enhancement and Chance Relief

Broadening is a crucial rule in establishing financial stability through land. The part investigates how spreading ventures across various property types and areas can relieve dangers and upgrade by and large portfolio versatility. Understanding gamble factors, leading expected level of investment, and having alternate courses of action are basic parts of a fruitful establishing financial stability procedure.

Long haul Vision and Versatility

Creating financial well-being through land requires a drawn-out vision and versatility to showcase changes. The section underscores the significance of remaining informed about market patterns, changing procedures when vital, and staying patient during market vacillations. The land is a developing scene, and a very much aligned approach guarantees supported development and abundance collection throughout the long term.

All in all, Section 9 gives an exhaustive guide to people looking to create financial well-being through land ventures and property on the board. By decisively moving toward ventures, utilising supporting and tax cuts, understanding property appreciation and income, dominating powerful property the executives, expanding portfolios, and keeping a drawn-out vision, pursuers are strategically situated to open the maximum capacity of land as a growing financial foundation instrument.

Strategies for success in a competitive market

In a cutthroat market, achievement requires a blend of vital reasoning, versatility, and a careful comprehension of the business scene. Part 9 of our aide gives perusers key systems to flourish in a cutthroat market climate.

Statistical Surveying and Knowledge

A central component of progress in a serious market is exhaustive statistical surveying. Section 9 urges perusers to dive into market patterns, purchaser conduct, and contender exercises. By remaining informed, organisations can distinguish holes, arising valuable open doors, and likely regions for separation, giving them an upper hand.

Separation and Special Incentive

Hanging out in a jam-packed market requests a reasonable and convincing one-of-a-kind offer. The part investigates systems for separation, stressing the significance of offering something novel or better than contenders. Whether it's through item development, prevalent client support, or extraordinary marking, organisations need to cut out a particular character.

Client Driven Approach

Focusing on a client-driven approach is a key methodology examined in Part 9. By getting it and addressing client needs, organisations can have areas of strength to fabricate and cultivate client faithfulness. Remarkable client encounters draw in new clients as well as add to rehash business and positive verbal exchange promoting.

Deftness and Flexibility

The outcome in a cutthroat market frequently depends on an organisation's capacity to adjust quickly to evolving conditions. The part investigates the idea of business spryness, empowering perusers to be proactive in answering business sector shifts. This could include changing item contributions, tweaking showcasing systems, or taking on new advances to remain in front of the opposition.

Vital Organizations and Joint efforts

Vital organisations can be an integral asset for outcomes in serious business sectors. Section 9 features the advantages of shaping collisions with correlative organisations, providers, or powerhouses. By utilising shared assets and organisations, organisations can extend their range and access new open doors, acquiring an upper hand.

Constant Development

Development is a main thrust in cutthroat business sectors, and the part focuses on the significance of cultivating a culture of ceaseless improvement. Whether through item development, process improvement, or taking on new advancements, organisations that embrace development position themselves as pioneers in their industry, drawing in clients looking for the most recent and best arrangements.

Vigorous Promoting and Marking

Powerful promoting and marking are investigated as fundamental parts of progress in a serious market. Part 9 aids perusers in creating convincing showcasing systems, using computerised stages, and building major areas of strength for a presence. Steady, designated informing assists organisations with slicing through the commotion and catching the consideration of their interest group.

Ability Securing and Maintenance

Getting and holding top ability is basic in a cutthroat market. The part examines techniques for drawing in talented experts, encouraging a positive work culture, and giving a continuous expert turn of events. A skilled and spurred labour force can be a critical resource in keeping an upper hand.

All in all, Section 9 outfits perusers with a complete arrangement of methodologies to explore and prevail in a cutthroat market. By putting resources into statistical surveying, separating contributions, focusing on consumer loyalty, embracing readiness, framing vital organisations, encouraging development, carrying out vigorous promoting, and supporting ability, organisations can situate themselves for supported progress despite wild rivalry.

Chapter 10:

Building a Supportive Network

In Part 10, the centre moves to the extraordinary force of building a strong organisation. Perceiving that achievement is many times a cooperative exertion, this section investigates the techniques and advantages of cultivating significant associations inside private and expert circles.

Organizing Procedures

The section jumps into successful systems administration techniques, accentuating the significance of credibility and certified relationship-building. Perusers gain bits of knowledge into developing a different organisation, utilising social stages, and exploring organising occasions with reason. Pragmatic tips are given to assist people with boosting the worth of their associations.

Proficient Mentorship

The meaning of mentorship is featured as a vital part of building a steady organisation. Whether looking for direction in a particular industry or exploring vocation choices, having guides can offer priceless bits of knowledge. Section 10 aids perusers on the most proficient method to distinguish possible tutors, lay out significant associations, and get the greatest advantage from coach-mentee connections.

Peer Backing and Cooperation

Building a strong organisation reaches out to past mentorship to incorporate companion backing and coordinated effort. This part investigates the advantages of teaming up with associates, industry friends, and similar people. From cultivating a cooperative workplace to partaking in bunch projects, perusers find how aggregate endeavours can prompt shared achievement.

Profound and Proficient Help

Perceiving that achievement isn't exclusively about proficient accomplishments, the part digs into the significance of basic encouragement inside an organisation. Building a strong organisation includes having people who figure out private difficulties and give support during both expert and individual achievements.

Web-based Systems administration and Advanced Presence

In the computerised age, web-based systems administration is an incredible asset, and Part 10 offers direction on developing a vigorous computerised presence. From improving LinkedIn profiles to participating in web-based networks, perusers figure out how to use innovation to extend their organisations and access open doors past geographic limits.

Supporting Connections

The part highlights the requirement for ceaseless exertion in sustaining connections inside an organisation. Systems for remaining associated, offering thanks, and are examined to offer help to other people. Building a steady organisation is a continuous cycle that flourishes with proportional connections and certifiable associations.

Organising for Business venture

For business visionaries and business experts, the section gives explicit experiences in systems administration to business development. From looking for expected financial backers to framing key organisations, perusers gain commonsense guidance on how systems administration assumes a vital part in the pioneering achievement.

Variety and Consideration

Perceiving the strength in variety, the section investigates the advantages of building an organisation that reflects changed viewpoints and foundations. Embracing variety and consideration enhances individual and expert encounters as well as adds to a stronger and more creative organisation.

All in all, Part 10 stresses that building a steady organisation is a foundation of progress, offering proficient open doors as well as constant reassurance and self-awareness. By utilising compelling systems administration procedures, looking for mentorship, teaming up with peers, supporting connections, and embracing variety, people can make a strong organisation that pushes them toward their objectives and goals.

Fostering connections, mentorship, and collaboration

Building an effective and satisfying profession frequently depends on the capacity to cultivate significant associations, take part in mentorship, and embrace cooperative open doors. This essential methodology is investigated top to bottom in Section 10, offering perusers experiences into the extraordinary force of these interconnected components.

Encouraging Associations

Section 10 features the meaning of developing a wide and different organisation. It goes past customary expert connections, underscoring the significance of valid associations. Whether going to systems administration occasions, drawing in with friends, or building connections on the web, the site gives reasonable guidance on sustaining associations that go past superficial corporations.

Mentorship for Proficient Development

Mentorship is introduced as an impetus for individual and expert turn of events. The section guides perusers on the most proficient method to search out tutors, fabricate significant associations with experienced people, and influence mentorship for important bits of knowledge and direction. Mentorship turns into a two-way road, helping both coach and mentee through shared encounters and information trade.

Cooperation as an Impetus

Cooperation is investigated as a strong power for development and achievement. Part 10 digs into how cooperative endeavours can prompt effective fixes, upgraded efficiency, and shared accomplishments. Perusers are urged to search out cooperative open doors, both inside their associations and through outer organisations, encouraging a climate of common help and shared achievement effectively.

The Job of The ability to understand individuals on a profound level

The capacity to understand people at their core is introduced as an urgent expertise in cultivating associations, mentorship, and cooperation. Understanding and exploring relational elements, remembering others' viewpoints, and imparting are talked about as key parts. The part offers bits of knowledge on creating the capacity to understand anyone on a profound level to effectively explore connections.

Online Stages and Computerised Joint Effort

Perceiving the developing idea of expert associations, Section 10 investigates the job of online stages and computerised joint effort instruments. From LinkedIn to virtual cooperation spaces, perusers gain experiences in utilising innovation for systems administration, mentorship, and cooperative tasks. The advanced scene grows the compass of associations and opens up new roads for cooperation.

Making a Culture of Coordinated Effort

For associations, the section gives direction on making a culture that cultivates coordinated effort. From initiative drives to group-building methodologies, the significance of imparting a cooperative outlook at all levels of an association is stressed. Building a cooperative culture improves representative commitment and hierarchical achievement.

Variety in Associations and Coordinated efforts

Recognizing the strength in variety, the section highlights the significance of developing associations and joint efforts that embrace changed viewpoints and foundations. Various organisations and cooperative groups are demonstrated to be stronger, more imaginative, and equipped for tending to complex difficulties.

All in all, Section 10 builds up the possibility that outcome in both individual and expert circles is altogether affected by the nature of associations, the direction from tutors, and the adequacy of cooperative endeavours. By encouraging true associations, looking for mentorship, embracing cooperative open doors, and supporting a culture that values variety, people and associations can open the maximum capacity of their organisations for supported achievement and development.

The importance of building a community for mutual growth and empowerment

Section 10 of our aid investigates the extraordinary force of building a local area — an aggregate of people joined by shared objectives, values, and a guarantee to common development and strengthening. This part highlights the various advantages gained from cultivating a feeling of the local area, both on an individual and expert level.

Shared Learning and Information Trade

Building a local area establishes a climate ready for shared learning and information trade. Individuals can draw upon one another's encounters, skills, and experiences, cultivating a persistent pattern of learning. This cooperative methodology speeds up private and aggregate development, as people contribute their exceptional viewpoints to the local area's aggregate pool of information.

Consistent reassurance and Strengthening

A feeling of the local area offers an urgent help framework. Part 10 investigates how a local area turns into a wellspring of basic encouragement during difficulties and triumphs. The common encounters inside the local area create a security that engages people to persist through troubles, celebrate triumphs, and beat impediments with an aggregate strength.

Organising Open doors and Cooperative energies

Networks are ripe grounds for systems administration, open doors, and cooperative energies. The section dives into how a very much associated local area opens ways to new coordinated efforts, organisations, and experts open doors. Through these organisations, people can get to a more extensive scope of assets, experiences, and potential joint efforts that add to individual and expert progression.

Aggregate Promotion and Impact

Joined people have an aggregate voice that can advocate for shared objectives and impact change. Whether it's inside an expert industry, social reason, or shared vested party, the section investigates how networks can impact positive change by preparing their aggregate impact. This feeling of aggregate promotion enables individuals to have a significant effect.

Variety and Inclusivity

Networks flourish with variety and inclusivity. The section highlights the significance of building networks that embrace people from different foundations, encouraging a rich embroidery of viewpoints. Comprehensive people groups establish conditions where everybody feels esteemed, heard, and enabled, adding to an additional lively and dynamic group.

Opportunities for Mentorship and Leadership

Inside a local area, mentorship and initiative open doors proliferate. Section 10 aids perusers on how networks give a rich ground to tutor mentee connections and initiative turn of events. People can both look for direction from experienced local area individuals and, thus, add to the development of others, making a pattern of mentorship and initiative.

Enhancing Accomplishment Through Aggregate Festival

Achievement turns out to be more significant when shared inside a local area. The section investigates how to aggregate festivals and enhance individual accomplishments. Locally, individuals elevate and praise each other's victories, making a positive and empowering environment that further energises everybody's inspiration and obligation to development.

All in all, Part 10 highlights the extraordinary effect of building a local area for shared development and strengthening. Whether in private or expert circles, the advantages of shared learning, consistent reassurance, organising, aggregate promotion, variety, mentorship, and aggregate festivals establish a climate where people can flourish together. Constructing and supporting a local area isn't simply a pathway to individual achievement but an excursion towards shared achievements and strengthening for every one of its individuals.

Conclusion

In the last pages of "Empowered Ventures: Business Ideas for Black Women," we end up at the convergence of motivation and plausibility. All through this enabling excursion, we've investigated inventive business thoughts, procedures for progress, and the significance of building a steady organisation.

As the pages go, it's obvious that the strength, versatility, and imagination of People of Colour business visionaries are considerable powers moulding the fate of the business. From imaginative undertakings to tech-driven adventures, the assorted business scene mirrors the unfathomable expectations that exist in the enterprising soul of Black women.

The book closes with a reverberating source of inspiration — to step into the universe of a business venture with certainty, to embrace the remarkable characteristics that put every lady aside, and to add to a tradition of strengthening that stretches out past individual achievement. May the narratives, thoughts, and experiences inside these pages act as both an aide and a wellspring of consolation. In each section, the message repeats: Your thoughts matter, your endeavours are important, and your process is one of importance.

As we bid goodbye to "Empowered Ventures," let it be an impetus for dreams sought after, challenges to survive, and organisations fabricated. The way ahead is enlightened by the common stories and aggregate insight inside these pages — a demonstration of the unprecedented potential inside each Person of colour business visionary. Here's to enabled adventures, limitless conceivable outcomes, and a future where the enterprising soul of People of colour proceeds to shape and rethink the business scene. May the excursion ahead be essentially as noteworthy and moving as the one we've left together inside the pages of this book.